The Ultimate Self-Teaching Method!   Level One

Play Accordion Today!

A Complete Guide to the Basics

By Gary Meisner

Recorded and produced by
Jim Reith at BeatHouse Music,
Milwaukee, WI

Stan Fomin, Audio Arrangements
Gary Meisner, Accordion
Joel Kopischke, Narration

PLAYBACK+
Speed • Pitch • Balance • Loop

To access audio, visit:
www.halleonard.com/mylibrary

Enter Code
1758-2225-8614-5184

ISBN 978-1-4234-9696-0

HAL•LEONARD®

E-Z Play® Today Music Notation © 1975 by HAL LEONARD CORPORATION
E-Z PLAY and EASY ELECTRONIC KEYBOARD MUSIC are registered trademarks of HAL LEONARD COR........ION.

Visit Hal Leonard Online at
www.halleonard.com

World headquarters, contact:
Hal Leonard
7777 West Bluemound Road
Milwaukee, WI 53213
Email: info@halleonard.com

In Europe, contact:
Hal Leonard Europe Limited
1 Red Place
London, W1K 6PL
Email: info@halleonardeurope.com

In Australia, contact:
Hal Leonard Australia Pty. Ltd.
4 Lentara Court
Cheltenham, Victoria, 3192 Australia
Email: info@halleonard.com.au

Introduction

Track 1

Welcome to *Play Accordion Today!* This book features a step-by-step learning approach to playing the accordion. There are 21 lessons. Each lesson explains and illustrates the music skills that will enable you to play a variety of songs. Whatever your goals are, *Play Accordion Today!* will give you the start you need.

About the Audio

To access the audio tracks, simply visit *www.halleonard.com/mylibrary* and enter the code from page 1 of this book. From here, you can stream or download all the audio tracks at your convenience.

It's easy and fun to play the accordion, and the accompanying audio will make your learning even more enjoyable as we take you through each lesson and play each song along with a full band. Much like a traditional lesson, the best way to learn this material is to read and practice a while on your own first, then listen to the audio. *Play Accordion Today!* is designed to help you learn at your own pace. If there is something you don't quite understand the first time through, go back to the track and listen again. Each musical track has been given a track number, so if you want to practice something again, you can find it right away.

Contents

Parts of the Accordion

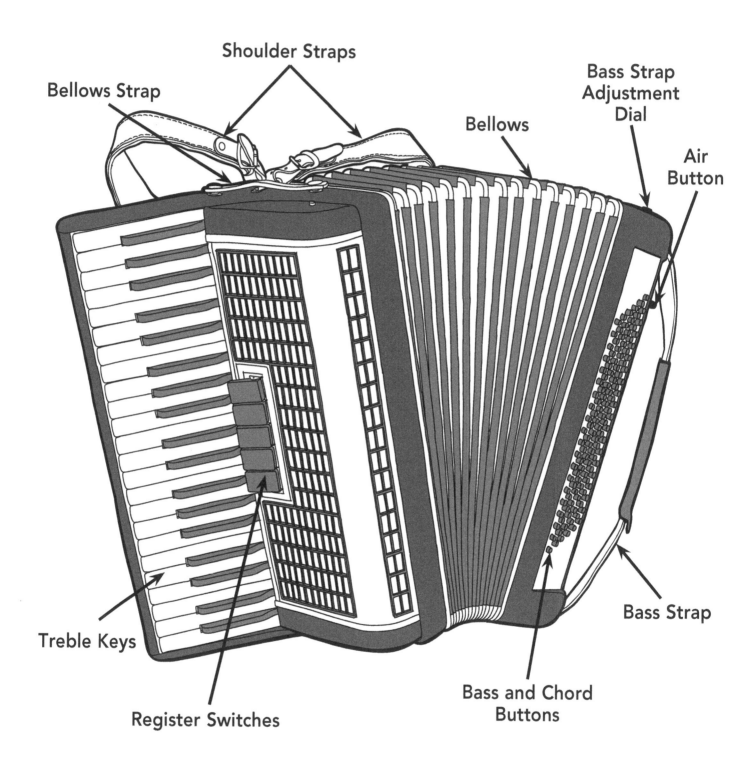

Shoulder Straps

Bellows Strap

Bass Strap Adjustment Dial

Bellows

Air Button

Treble Keys

Bass Strap

Register Switches

Bass and Chord Buttons

- **Treble Keys** – There are 41 treble keys on most standard accordions. The black keys are arranged in alternating groups of two and three, just like the piano.

- **Bass and Chord Buttons** – The standard accordion has 120 buttons arranged in six rows. The two rows closest to the bellows are bass notes. The remaining four rows are chords.

- **Shoulder Straps** – Adjust the shoulder straps to a comfortable position. For added stability, a back strap may also be used. The back strap has two pieces. Each piece attaches to a shoulder strap and then hooks together to provide better support.

- **Air Button** – This button releases air so you can close the bellows without making any sounds.

- **Bellows Straps** – These straps keep the bellows closed so it's easier to take the instrument in and out of the case.

- **Register Switches** – These switches change the sound by controlling which reeds are opened or closed.

- **Bellows** – The bellows are the heart and soul of the accordion. Reeds are activated when the bellows are pushed and pulled. By controlling the flow of air, you can make the music louder or softer (called *dynamics*).

- **Bass Strap and Bass Strap Adjustment Dial** – The bass strap helps you move the bellows in and out by bracing your hand. Use the adjustment dial at the top of the strap to make it tighter or looser.

Track 2

The Treble Keyboard

The standard accordion has 41 treble keys which are played by the right hand. Play various keys on the keyboard while slowly moving the bellows in and out. Notice how the pitch gets higher when you move down toward the floor, and lower when you move up closer to your chin.

Now, refer to the following illustration and locate Middle C. You will play this note with your thumb, D with your second finger, E with your third finger, F with your fourth finger and G with your fifth finger. Play each note separately, keeping your fingers curved.

Notice that the black keys occur in alternating groups of two and three. The first note that you played was Middle C, which is located just before the first group of two black keys. You can use Middle C as a "landmark" to help you find other notes.

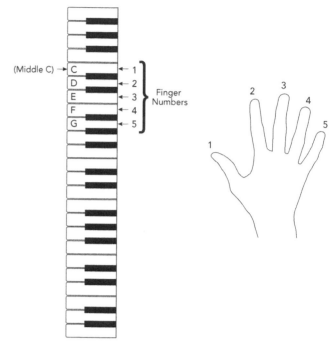

Let's play a familiar melody with the five notes you've just learned.

Ode to Joy

Track 3

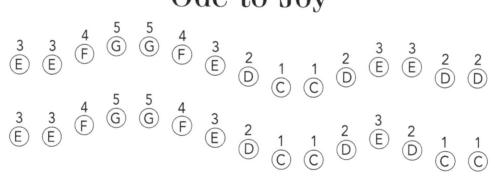

Here's another well-known melody using the same five notes. Hum along as you play.

Mary Had a Little Lamb

Track 4

Track 5

How to Read Music

Time Values

As you played "Mary Had a Little Lamb," did you notice that some notes were held longer than others? The period of time that a note is held is measured in **beats**. Here are four common types of notes and their time values.

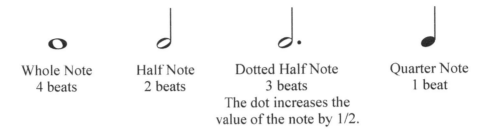

Whole Note	Half Note	Dotted Half Note	Quarter Note
4 beats	2 beats	3 beats	1 beat

The dot increases the value of the note by 1/2.

In written music, each note tells you which key or button to play, and also how long it should be held.

The Staff

Music is written on a **staff**. The staff has five lines and four spaces.

The staff is divided into sections called **measures**.

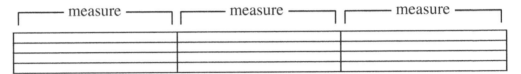

The Treble Clef

Track 6

A clef sign appears at the beginning of the staff. This is the **treble clef** (sometimes called the G clef).

In treble clef, the names of the lines and spaces are as follows:

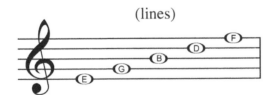

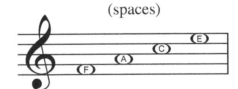

Ledger Lines

Sometimes short lines are added above or below the staff to accommodate additional notes. These are called **ledger lines**.

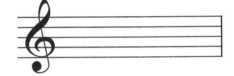

The Time Signature

After the clef sign you'll find a **time signature**, which consists of two numbers. The top number tells you how many beats are in each measure, and the bottom number tells you which kind of note gets one beat.

Let's put all of these music basics to work by playing "When the Saints Go Marching In." This song uses the same five notes you've already learned. Play slowly at first.

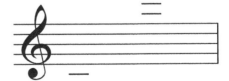

four beats in a measure

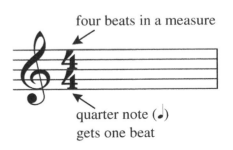

quarter note (♩) gets one beat

7

Here's how these five notes look on the staff.

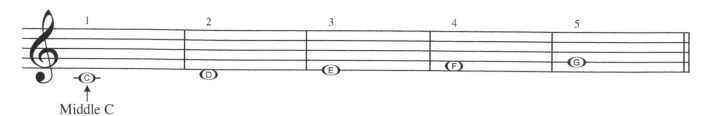

Middle C

Track 7

When the Saints Go Marching In
(Right-Hand Version)

Pickup Notes: Incomplete measure at the beginning of a song. The missing beats are usually found at the end.

Tie: Two notes tied together. In this case the whole note plus the quarter note equals 5 counts.

The Bass and Chord Section

Track 8

The buttons in the bass and chord section normally play the accompaniment to the melody. The standard bass and chord section (Stradella) has 120 buttons arranged in six rows. The first two rows (closest to the bellows) are single tones and the remaining four rows are chords. When a chord button is played, three or more notes sound simultaneously. The following example shows the function of each of the six rows of buttons:

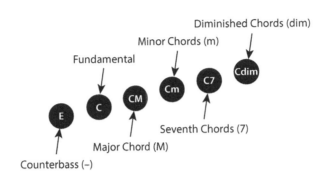

Insert your left hand through the bass strap. Be sure it fits snugly. Use the bass strap adjustment dial to change the strap length if needed.

The fingers of your left hand are numbered from 1 to 5. You will use fingers 2-5 to play the bass and chord section.

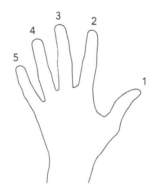

Find the C guide button, which is usually concave but sometimes has a rhinestone insert (your instrument may have additional guide buttons). The C guide button is in the fundamental row, near the center of the button area. Put your 3rd finger on C and your 2nd finger on the button behind it. This is the C Major chord button.

Track 9

Now, play the following example. Each bass note and chord gets one beat. Use your 3rd finger on the bass note and your 2nd finger on the chord.

TIP: For the best effect, play the bass notes and chords short and crisp.

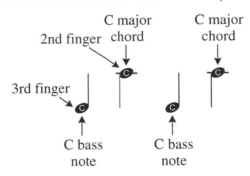

9

How to Read Bass and Chord Notation

Let's learn a few more bass notes and chords. Start by locating the following buttons.

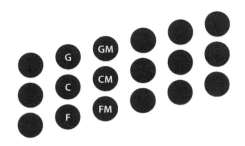

Track 10

Now, play the following example. (C, G, and F are all major chords.)

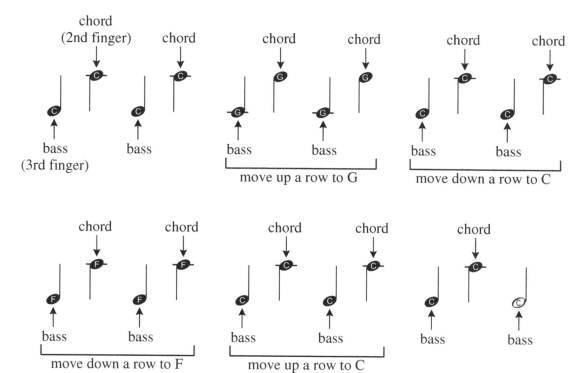

Track 11

The Bass Clef

The notes in the bass and chord section are written in the **bass clef** (sometimes called the F clef).

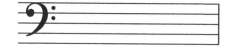

The lines and spaces in bass clef are named as follows. Notice that they are named differently than they are in treble clef.

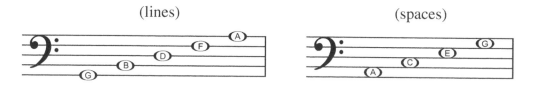

Here's how the example you played on page 10 looks when written in bass clef.

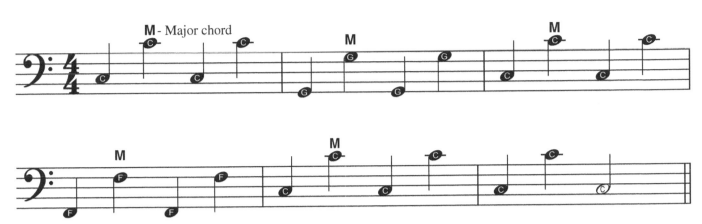

Track 12

Now, let's add a simple melody to this bass part and play with both hands together. Notice that the treble and bass clef staves have been combined. This is called the **grand staff**.

Generally, bass notes are written on or below the 3rd staff line, while chords are written above the 3rd staff line. It is necessary to extend the bass clef staff with ledger lines to accommodate all the notes you'll be playing. The following diagram shows commonly used notes for the accompaniment.

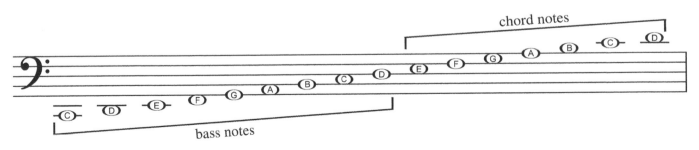

Ties

A tie is a curved line connecting two notes on the same line or space. Hold the first note for the combined time value of all tied notes.

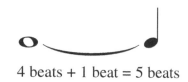

4 beats + 1 beat = 5 beats

Pickup Notes

When the time value of the notes at the beginning of a song does not equal a full measure, these notes are called pickup notes. The missing beats of that measure are usually found at the end of the song.

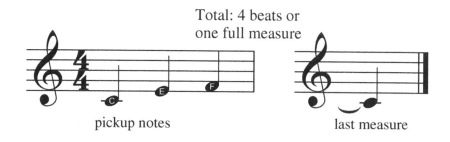

Rests

Rests are periods of silence in music. Like notes, they have definite time values.

Quarter rest 𝄽 = 1 beat

Half rest ▬ = 2 beats

Whole rest ▬ = 4 beats or one full measure of silence.

Chord symbols (C, G, F, etc.) will be used throughout this book, starting with your next song. These symbols are a type of musical shorthand which tells you at a glance what chords to play. When a chord letter appears without any other indication, it is a major chord (M). You'll learn about other types of chords later.

Track 13

When the Saints Go Marching In
(Full Version)

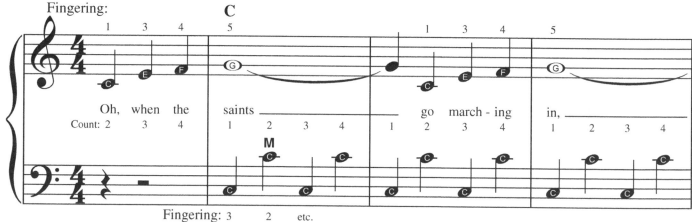

New Note: A

Track 14

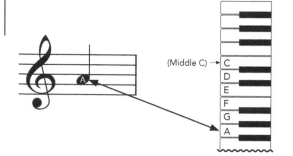

(Middle C) →

The melody for "Kum Ba Yah" uses six notes instead of the five you've been playing. Pay close attention to the marked fingering as you move out of the five-finger position and play the A note. There is also one new fingering technique:

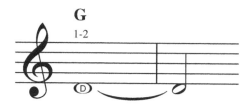

The "1-2" fingering means to play D with your thumb, and then—without releasing the note—change to the second finger.

Play the bass and chord together in the last measure.

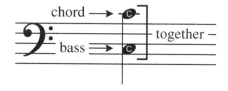

Kum Ba Yah

Track 15

half rest

bass and chord
together

Tempo and Dynamic Marks

At the beginning of each song you'll find a *tempo mark* and a *dynamic mark*. Here are a few tempo mark examples:

Moderately
Slowly
Lively

Dynamic marks tell you how loud or soft you should play. This is controlled by changing the flow of air in the bellows. Pushing or pulling harder on the bellows will increase the volume, and vice versa.

Here are the most common dynamic marks. These symbols are based on Italian terms, which are shown in parentheses.

pp – very soft (*pianissimo*)

p – soft (*piano*)

mf – medium loud (*mezzo forte*)

f – loud (*forte*)

ff – very loud (*fortissimo*)

"Michael, Row the Boat Ashore" is another melody with six notes. Here's another fingering technique:

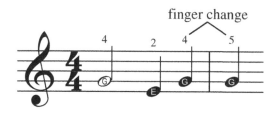

Michael, Row the Boat Ashore

Track 16

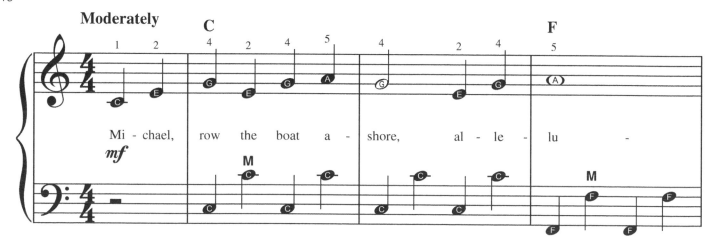

New Note: B

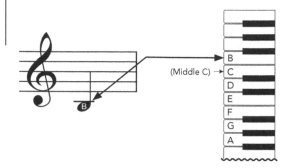

In "Marianne," you'll play B, which is located next to Middle C. Notice that it sounds lower in pitch but is located higher on the keyboard.

Seventh (7) Chords

All of the chords you have played so far have been major (M) chords. Now you will move back to the seventh (7) chord row and play G7. Use your 4th finger on the bass note and your 2nd finger on the seventh (7) chord.

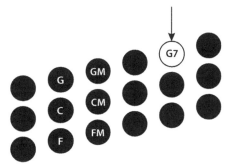

Before playing "Marianne," practice the following example until you are comfortable with moving from C and CM to G and G7. Play slowly at first.

Track 17

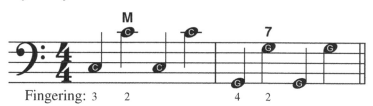

Fingering: 3   2   4   2

Track 18

Marianne

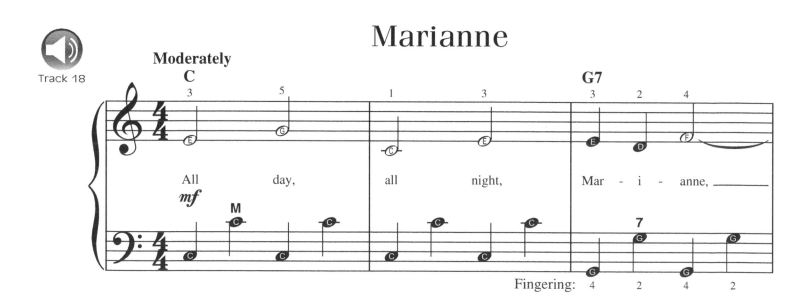

Fingering: 4   2   4   2

¾ Time Signature

"Beautiful Brown Eyes" is written in ¾ time.

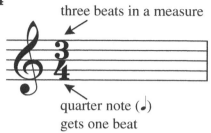

three beats in a measure

quarter note (♩)
gets one beat

Track 19

Play the following example. Notice that there is one bass note and two chords in each measure.

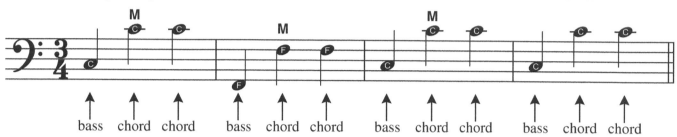

bass chord chord   bass chord chord   bass chord chord   bass chord chord

Counterbass

The counterbass row is the first row in the bass and chord section, closest to the bellows. Like the fundamental bass notes, they also produce single tones. Notes in the counterbass row are indicated with a line under the note.

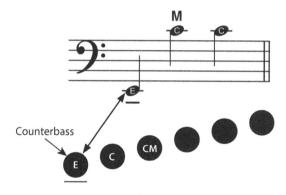

Counterbass

NOTE: From now on, finger numbers will not appear on every note.

Track 20

Beautiful Brown Eyes

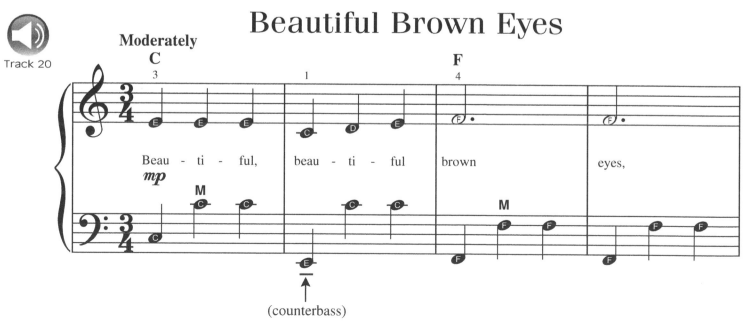

Moderately

Beau - ti - ful,   beau - ti - ful   brown   eyes,

mp

(counterbass)

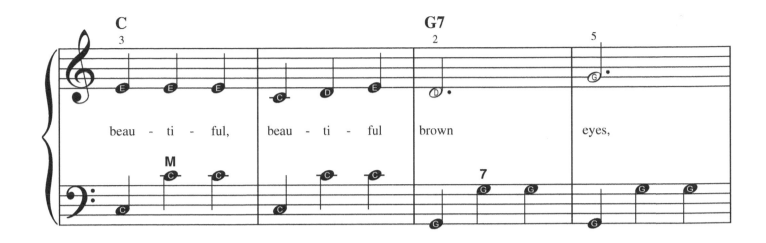

beau - ti - ful, beau - ti - ful brown eyes,

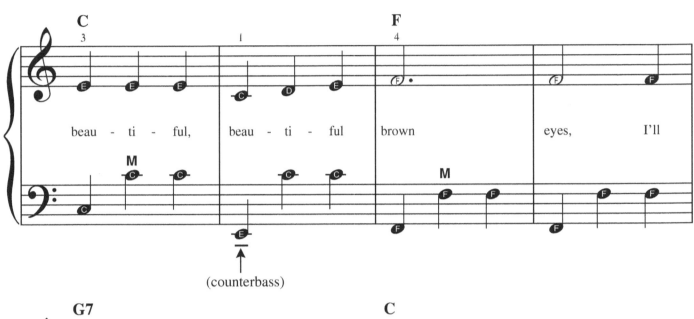

beau - ti - ful, beau - ti - ful brown eyes, I'll

(counterbass)

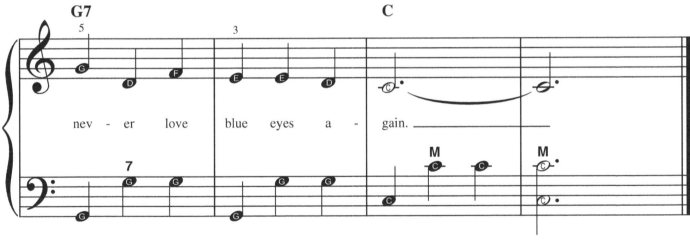

nev - er love blue eyes a - gain. _____

New Note: A

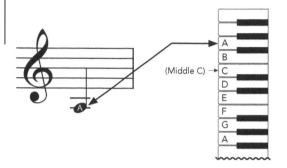

This new note is two white keys lower in pitch than Middle C, but higher on the keyboard.

Half Steps

The distance between two adjacent keys is called a *half step*. The different types of half steps are shown in this illustration:

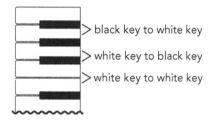

> black key to white key

> white key to black key

> white key to white key

Sharps and Flats

When a sharp ♯ sign appears next to a note, raise the note one half step. When a flat ♭ sign appears next to a note, lower the note one half step. Sharps and flats remain in effect for the duration of a measure.

You'll find one D♯ in the next song, "Maori Farewell Song" (p. 24–25). Locate and circle it in the music.

A natural ♮ sign cancels a sharp or flat.

Minor Chords

The minor chord row is located behind the major chord row. Minor chords are indicated with a lowercase "m." You'll play one Fm chord in "Maori Farewell Song." Locate and circle it in the music.

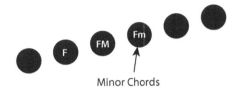

Minor Chords

Use your 3rd finger on the bass note and your 2nd finger on the minor chord.

New Chords: D7 and A7

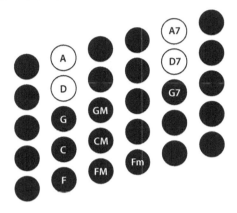

Track 21

Locate the new chords and play the following example:

Remember: When playing seventh (7) chords, use your 4th finger on the bass note and your 2nd finger on the chord.

Repeat Signs

Repeat signs make it possible to shorten printed music without changing the length of the song. They usually appear in sets of two.

There will be one repeat sign at the beginning of the section to be repeated. Play up to the repeat sign at the end of this section. Go back to the first repeat sign and play the section again. If there is no repeat sign to go back to, return to the beginning of the song.

Endings

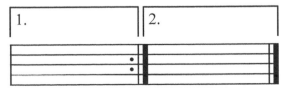

When two different endings occur in a song, here's what to do:

- Play the song through the 1st ending.
- Go back to the closest repeat sign, or back to the beginning.
- Play that section again, skip the first ending, and play the 2nd ending.

Maori Farewell Song

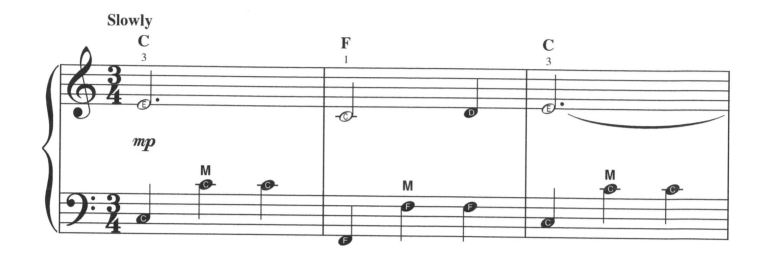

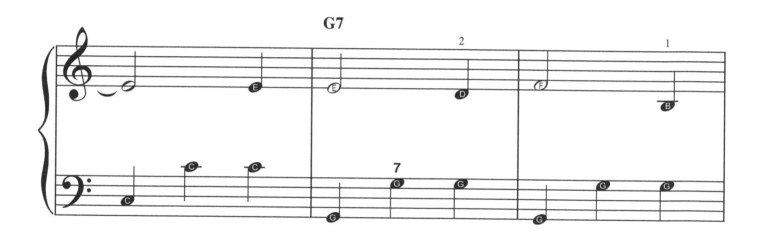

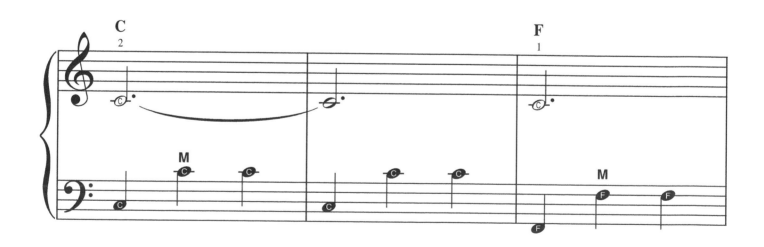

Key Signatures

Some songs that you'll play from now on will have one or more sharps or flats written at the beginning of each staff of music. These sharps and flats are known as the *key signature.* The word "key" represents the key note or basic note around which the other tones of a song are organized.

All of the songs you've played so far have had no sharps or flats in their key signature. These songs have all been in the key of C. In the song "Aura Lee," a sharp sign appears on the F line of both the treble and bass staves. This tells you that each F should be played as F♯, and the song is in the key of G.

New Notes: B and C

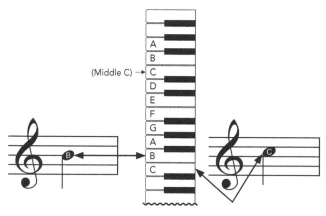

New Chord: E7

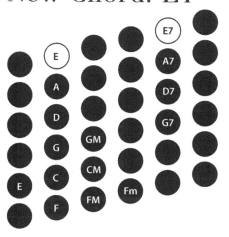

Aura Lee

Track 23

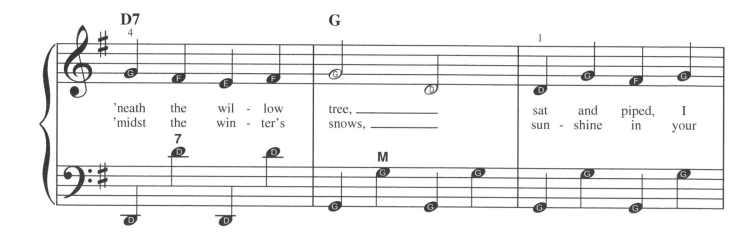

Key of F

In the song "The Bear Went Over the Mountain," a flat sign appears on the B line of both the treble and bass staves. This tells you that each B should be played as B♭, and the song is in the key of F.

New Chords: B♭, C7, and F7

Track 24

Locate these chords in the bass and chord section diagram.

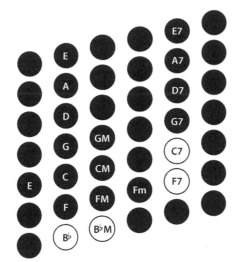

Practice this example until you are comfortable with the new chords.

New Note: High D

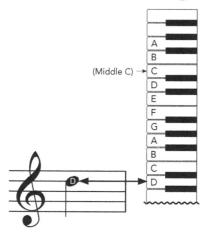

Locate and play the new D note.

The Bear Went Over the Mountain

Track 25

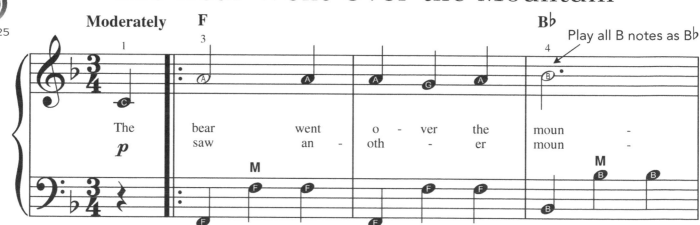

The bear went o - ver the moun -
saw an - oth - er moun -

28

tain.   The   bear   went   o - ver   the   moun -
tain.   He   saw   an -   oth   -   er   moun -

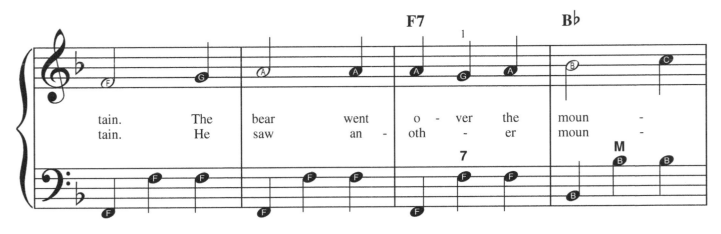

tain.   The   bear   went   o - ver   the   moun -
tain.   He   saw   an -   oth   -   er   moun -

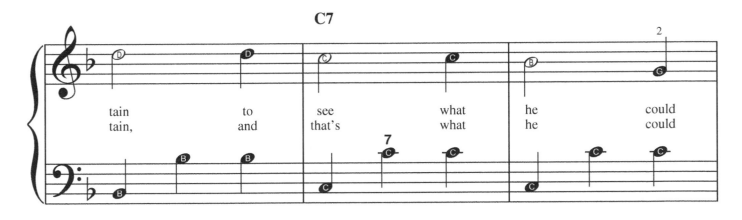

tain   to   see   what   he   could
tain,   and   that's   what   he   could

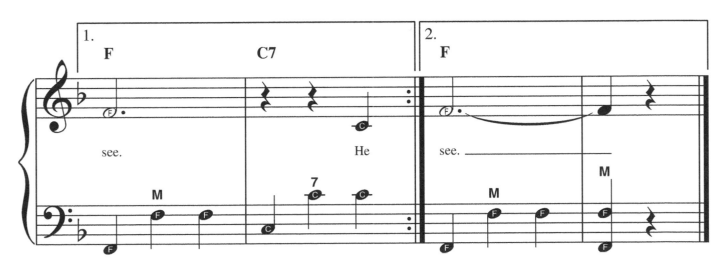

see.   He   see. _____

Eighth Notes

So far, you've learned four different types of notes—whole, half, dotted half, and quarter. In "The Alphabet Song," you'll learn how to play eighth notes.

Single eighth notes look like a quarter note with a flag on the stem.

Eighth notes that are written in groups of two or four are connected by a beam.

Eighth notes receive 1/2 beat. Therefore, it takes two eighth notes to equal one full beat.

$$\text{♫} = \text{♩} = 1 \text{ beat}$$

Track 26

Eighth notes are played twice as fast as quarter notes. The following example shows how each beat is divided into two parts saying the word "and" between each number. Count aloud as you play this example.

1 & 2 & 3 & 4 &   1 & 2 & 3 & 4 &

The following measure is taken from "The Alphabet Song" on the next page.

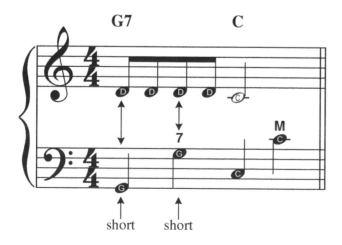

TIP: Bass notes and chords are usually played short and crisp for the best effect. In the example to the left, play the G bass on the first eighth note and the G7 chord on the third D eighth note. (The second and fourth eighth notes are played alone.)

The Alphabet Song

Fast

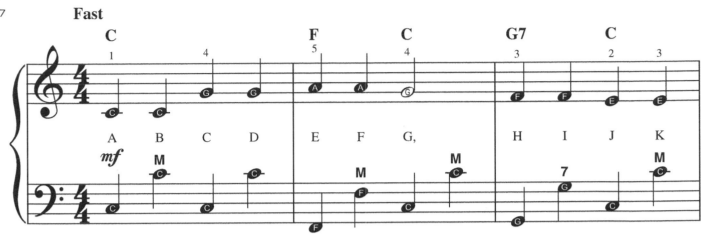

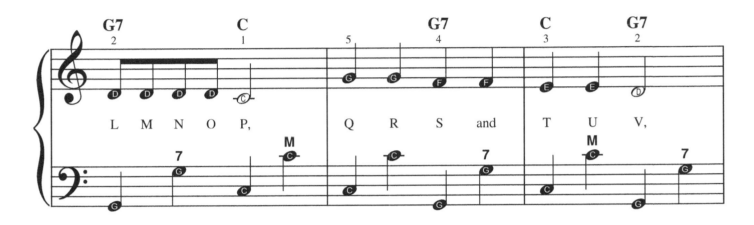

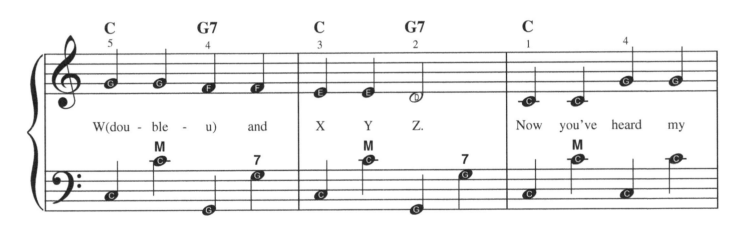

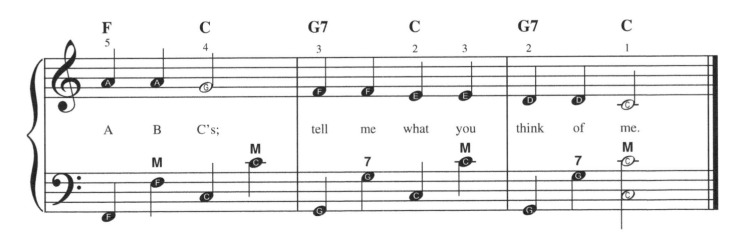

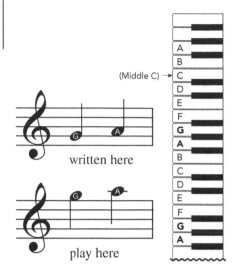

(Middle C) →

written here

play here

When an *8va* sign is written over a group of notes, it means that you should play those notes one octave higher. An octave is the distance from any key to the next key having the same name (G to G, for example).

To cancel the *8va* sign, the Italian term *loco* is often used. This word instructs you to play the notes where they are written.

Bass Solo

In the introduction of "Julida Polka," you'll see a measure with bass notes only and no chords. Practice this measure until you are comfortable with the bass note movement.

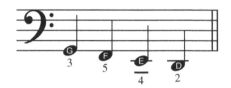

Julida Polka

Track 28

New Chords: Em and Am

Locate these chords on the following diagram.

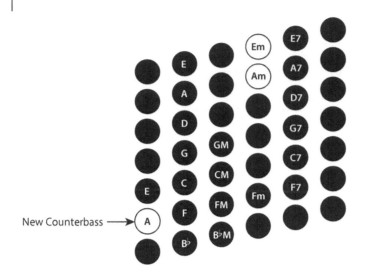

New Counterbass ⟶

 Track 29

Now, play the following example to become familiar with the move from CM to Am and CM to Em.

New Bass Accompaniment

In the second half of "The Caissons Go Rolling Along" (p. 36-37), notice that the accompaniment pattern changes. Now the bass notes and chords are played together, which creates an added march-like effect. Practice this accompaniment in the following example.

Track 30

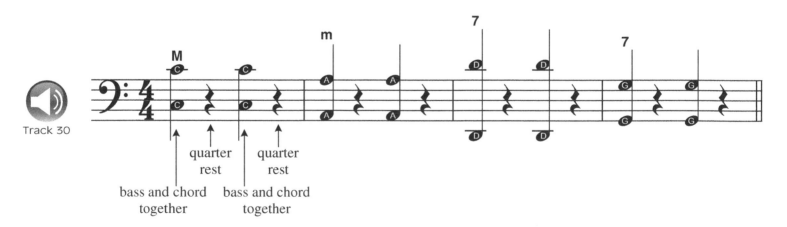

quarter rest   quarter rest

bass and chord together   bass and chord together

Accordion Registration

From now on, you'll see a round diagram at the beginning of each song for both the treble keyboard and the bass and chord section. Here are some examples:

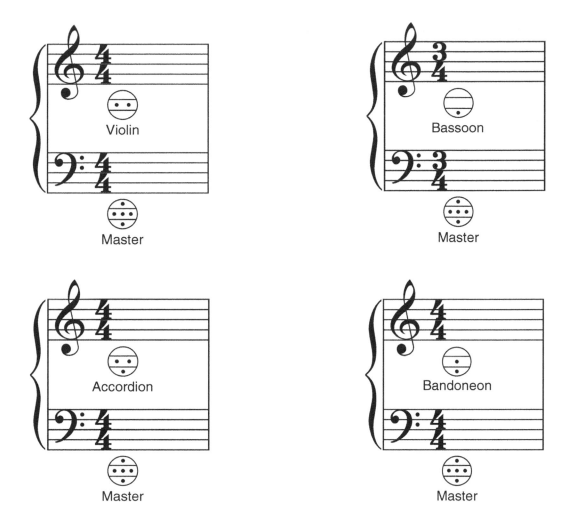

The number of available switches varies, depending on the make and model of your accordion.

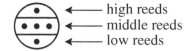

— high reeds
— middle reeds
— low reeds

Registrations are only suggestions. Experiment and use the sounds that are pleasing to you. Also, don't hesitate to change registrations within a song to create an entirely different effect!

Track 31

The Caissons Go Rolling Along

36

New Notation

Now that you've become more familiar with reading music, letter names will no longer appear inside the notes. Instead, these names will be placed to the left of the notes as a reminder. When identical notes appear consecutively, you'll only see a letter on the first note. Letter names for the bass accompaniment are written at the beginning, and then every time there is a different bass and chord. Here's an example:

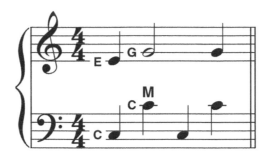

Dotted Quarter Notes

As you learned with dotted half notes, a dot placed after any note increases its time value by one half. For example, a dotted half note receives three beats. The same principle applies to the dotted quarter note.

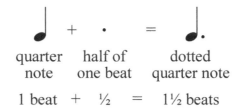

quarter note   half of one beat   dotted quarter note

1 beat + ½ = 1½ beats

A dotted quarter note is usually followed by an eighth note. The following example is taken from "She Wore a Yellow Ribbon." Notice that the eighth note following the dotted quarter note is played without a bass note or chord.

Play this example several times to get the "feel" of how the right and left hands are coordinated. Don't forget to count!

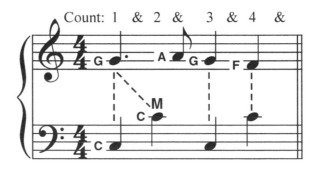

She Wore a Yellow Ribbon

Lively

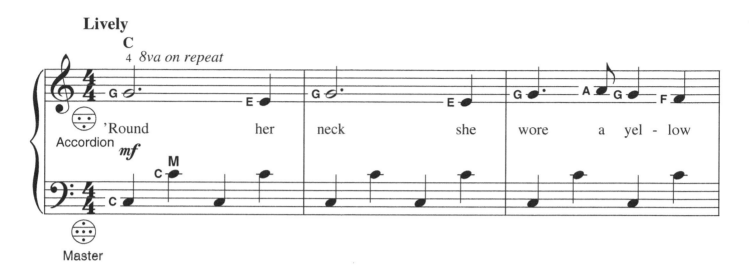

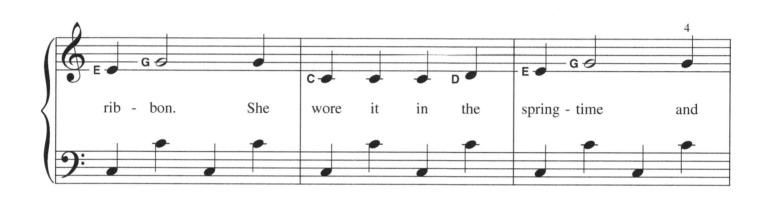

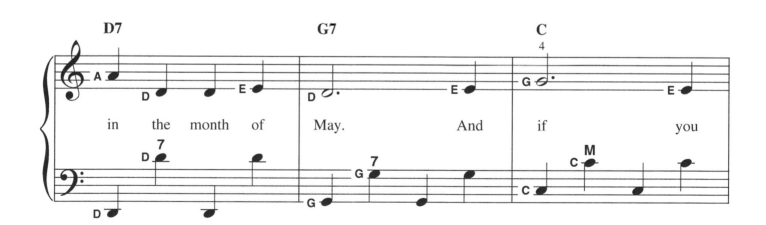

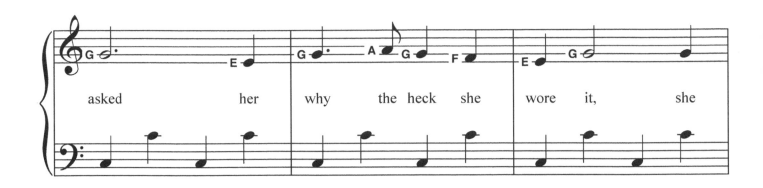

asked her why the heck she wore it, she

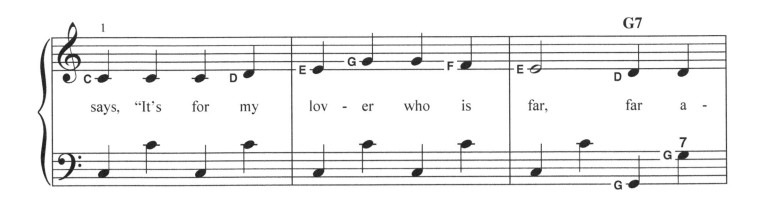

says, "It's for my lov - er who is far, far a -

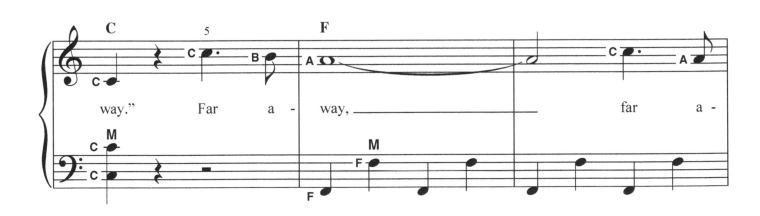

way." Far a - way, ____ far a -

way. ____ She wore it for her

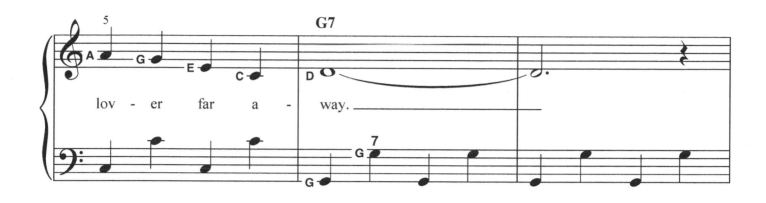

lov - er far a - way. _____

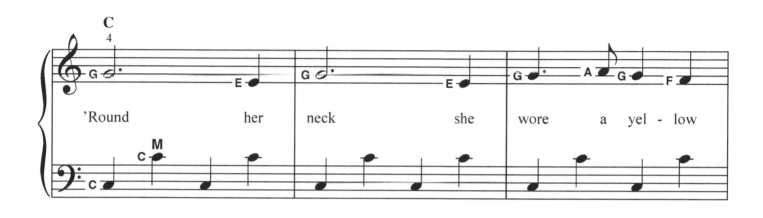

'Round   her   neck   she   wore   a   yel - low

rib - bon.   She   wore   it   for   her   lov - er   who   is

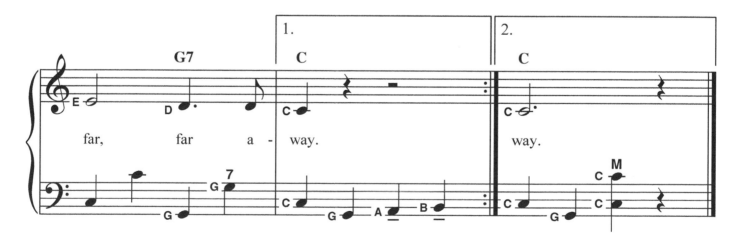

far,   far   a - way.   way.

New Note: High E

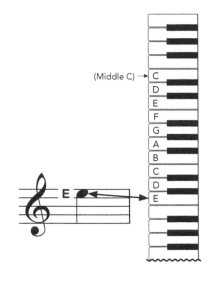

Double Notes

Until now, you've played all single melody notes. To create a fuller sound, double notes have been included in the arrangement of "Little Brown Jug." Generally, the top note is the melody, while the lower note adds harmony. Play the following example to familiarize yourself with this technique.

New Bass Pattern

In the following song, the usual $\frac{4}{4}$ pattern of bass-chord-bass-chord has been slightly altered to bass-chord-chord-chord. Here's how it looks on the staff:

Little Brown Jug

Track 33

Lively

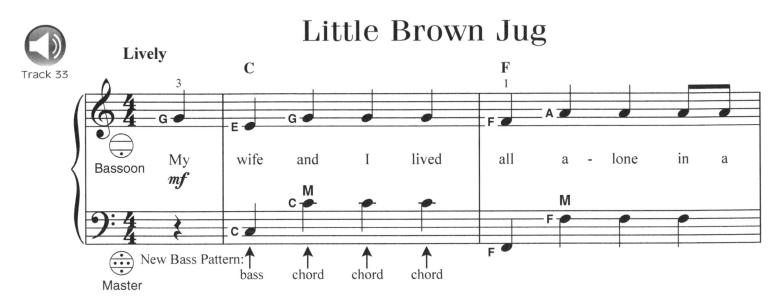

My wife and I lived all a - lone in a

Bassoon
mf

Master

New Bass Pattern: bass chord chord chord

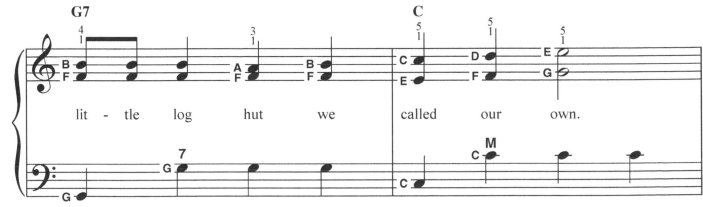

lit - tle log hut we called our own.

New Fingering Technique

As the songs you play become more advanced, this technique will help you to play more smoothly. The following example illustrates how to "cross under" and "cross over." Notice that you will cross under as you move up the keyboard and cross over as you move down the keyboard.

Fermata Sign 𝄐

A fermata sign indicates that you may hold that note or chord longer than its original time value. Fermatas are used to add emphasis, as in the final measure of "Scarborough Fair," shown below.

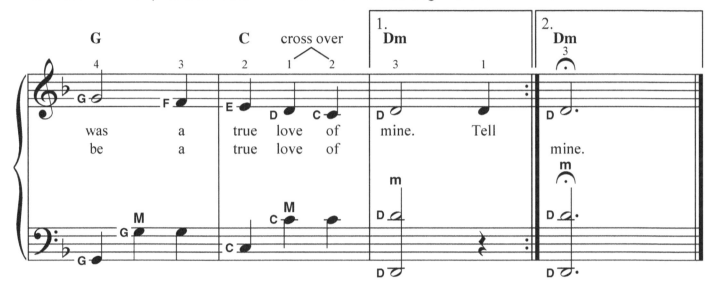

New Chord: Dm

Refer to the chart on page 63 to locate and play the new Dm chord above.

Track 34

Scarborough Fair

44

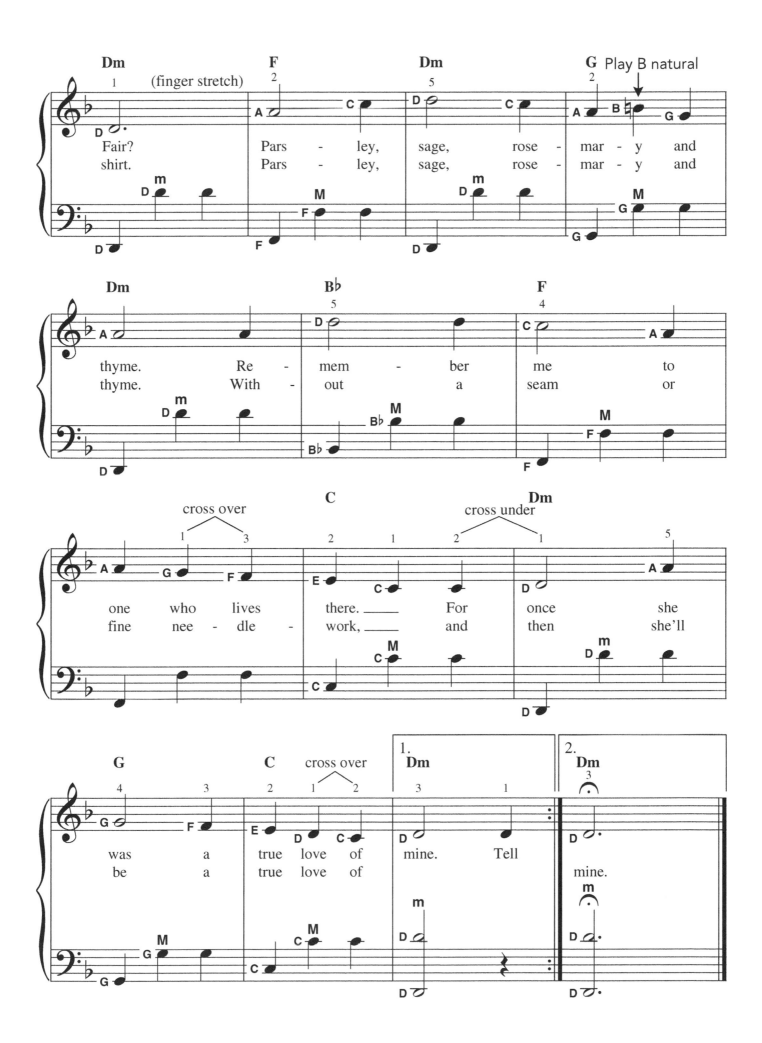

New Rhythm Pattern

This new pattern is similar to the bass-chord-bass-chord rhythm you've been playing. For this pattern, play two eighth-note chords on the 2nd beat of each measure, as illustrated in the following example. Be sure to count as you play!

Track 35

For a variation on this pattern, add another chord on the 4th beat.

Track 36

New Chord: Gm

Locate and play the Gm chord. Refer to the chart on page 63 if needed.

Track 37

St. James Infirmary

46

Standard Notation

Now you're ready to take off the training wheels! Take a look at "Bill Bailey" on page 50. This is the first song where no note names are included. You'll also notice that the size of the staff and the notes have been reduced slightly. This is called standard notation. Feel free to refer back to the names of the lines and spaces if needed (pages 7 and 10).

Alternating Basses

So far, the name of the chord has been the same as the bass note. For example, when you played the CM chord, you played a C bass note; when you played the G7 chord, you played a G bass note. Now, to add interest to the bass accompaniment, bass notes other than the name of the chord will be added to the bass part. These are called alternating basses.

In this case, the alternating bass is up one button from the fundamental bass.

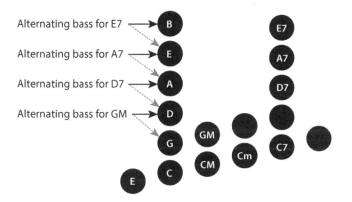

Play the following example from "Bill Bailey." Note names for the bass notes have been included. Use the indicated fingering.

Track 38

Naturals

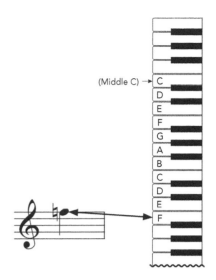

As a reminder, the natural ♮ sign cancels out a sharp or flat. Since "Bill Bailey" is in the key of G, all the F notes are usually sharp. When a melody in the key of G has an F note that is *not* sharp, a natural sign is used. Locate the new high F note.

Extended Endings (or Tags)

The ending to "Bill Bailey" is four measures longer than usual. In this case, the extended ending is simply a repeat of the last four measures of the song. These measures create a more dramatic finish to the tune.

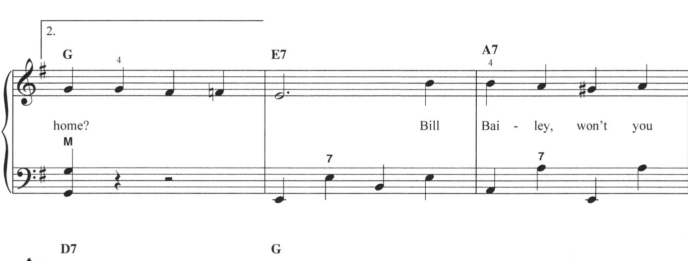

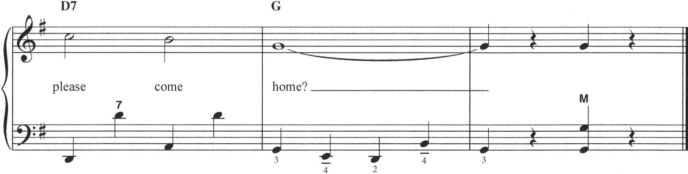

Bill Bailey, Won't You Please Come Home

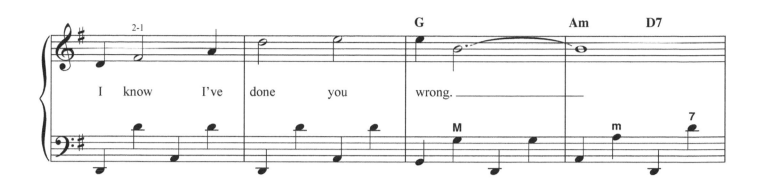

I know I've done you wrong.

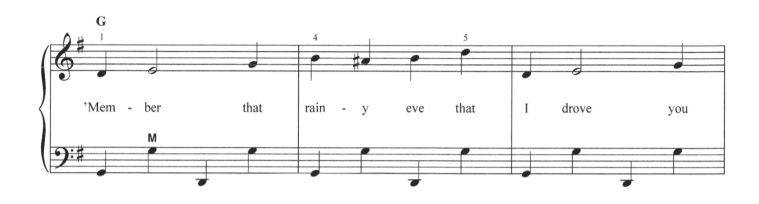

'Mem - ber that rain - y eve that I drove you

out, with noth - in' but a fine tooth

comb? I know I'm to

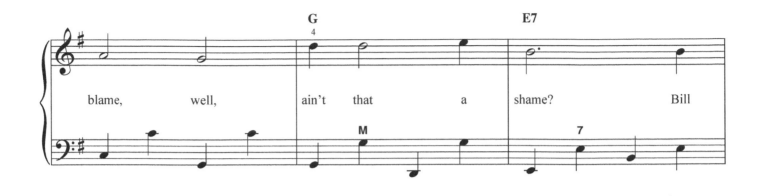

blame,   well,   ain't that   a   shame?   Bill

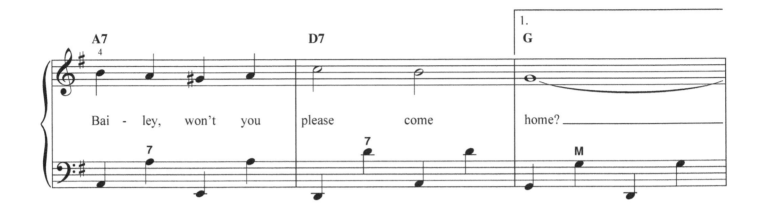

Bai - ley, won't you   please   come   home? _____

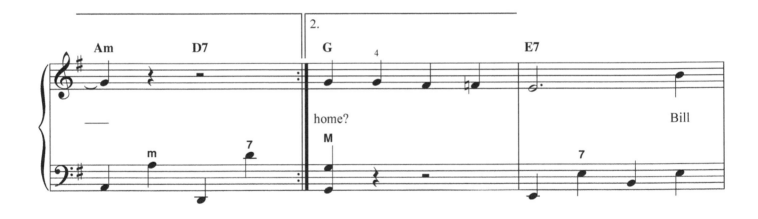

_____   home?   Bill

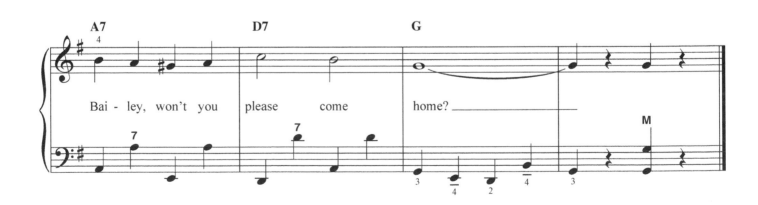

Bai - ley, won't you   please   come   home? _____

Syncopation

Syncopation is the technique of playing a melody note or notes on the "weak" beats of the measure. For example, instead of playing a note on a strong beat such as 1, 2, 3, or 4, the note is played on the "and" eighth note.

Play the following syncopated rhythm. Be sure to count!

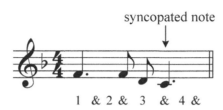

1 & 2 & 3 & 4 &

Glissando

The term *glissando* (or *gliss* for short) means "gliding" or "sliding." To play a glissando down the keyboard (up in pitch), turn your hand slightly and use the nail of your index or middle finger to slide across the white keys. Press hard enough to play each note in turn, but slide quickly enough so that the notes blend into a single "whoosh."

In printed music, a glissando is indicated by a wavy line between notes. The following example is taken from the last measure of the next song, "Swing Low, Sweet Chariot."

Swing Eighth Notes

Generally, "swing" refers to notes with equal time values played with unequal durations. In the next song, you'll have an opportunity to "swing" the eighth notes.

Here's how: First, play this pattern evenly.

Track 40

Now play it with a swing feel.

Track 41

long short long short long short long

53

Swing Low, Sweet Chariot

Moderately, with a swing feel

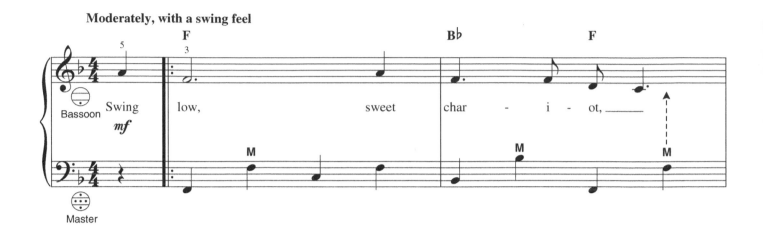

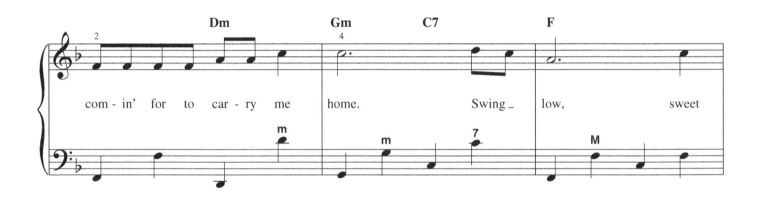

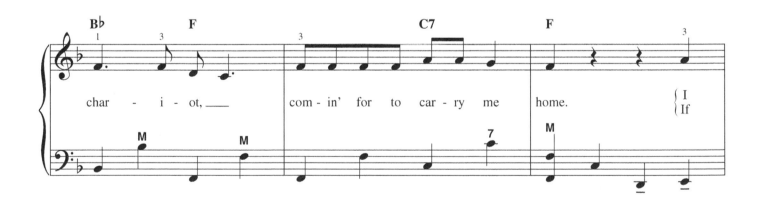

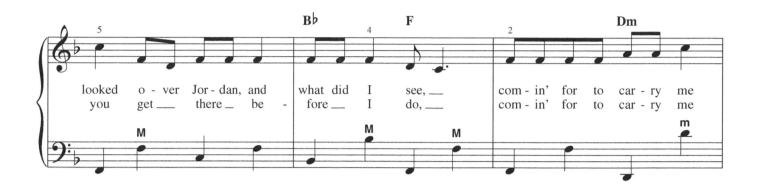

looked o - ver Jor - dan, and | what did I see, ___ | com - in' for to car - ry me
you get ___ there ___ be - | fore ___ I do, ___ | com - in' for to car - ry me

home? A | band ___ of an - gels | com - in' af - ter me, ___
home, tell | all ___ my friends I'm a - | com - in',_____ too, ___

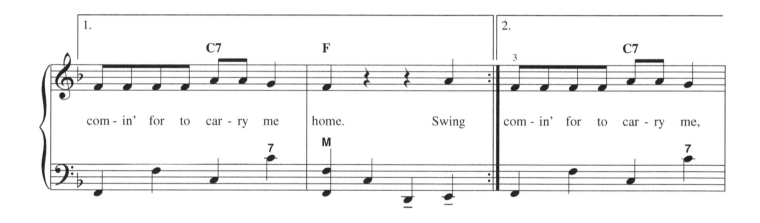

com - in' for to car - ry me | home. Swing | com - in' for to car - ry me,

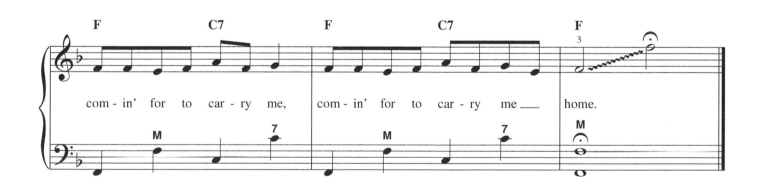

com - in' for to car - ry me, | com - in' for to car - ry me ___ | home.

Countermelody

In the second section of "Chiapanecas," there is a secondary melody played by the left hand. This is known as a *countermelody*. It adds interest and support to the main melody played by the right hand.

Remember: You can always refer to the Bass and Chord Chart on page 63 for the location of specific buttons.

Chiapanecas

Track 43

(countermelody)

Right-Hand Chords

For the first time in this book, you'll now play chords with your right hand. As you may remember from Lesson 2, a chord consists of three or more notes sounding together. Practice the following examples, taken from "Peg o' My Heart."

Peg o' My Heart

Track 44

eighth rest

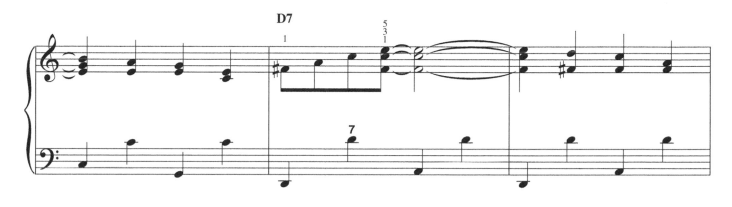

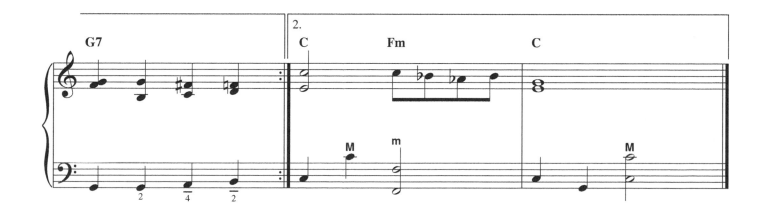

Key of B♭

The key signature of B♭ has two flats—B♭ and E♭. All B and E notes are flat unless canceled by a natural ♮ sign.

New Chords: Cm, E♭, and B♭7

Locate these new chords using the chart on page 63.

Sustained Accompaniment

The bass and chord part for "America, the Beautiful" consists of mostly half notes. This creates a hymn-like effect for this wonderful song.

Diminished Chords

There is one diminished chord (Fdim) in "America, the Beautiful." Diminished chords are located in the last row of chord buttons. They are indicated by the abbreviation "dim."

Use your 4th finger for the bass note and your 2nd finger for the Fdim chord.

Ritardando

The musical term *rit.* appears in the last measure of "America, the Beautiful." This is an abbreviation for the Italian word *ritardando*, which means to gradually slow down. This creates a more dramatic finish to your song.

Track 45

America, the Beautiful

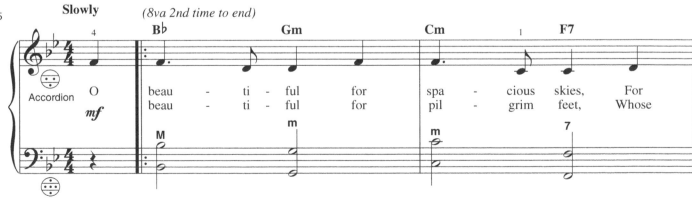

Treble Keyboard Chart

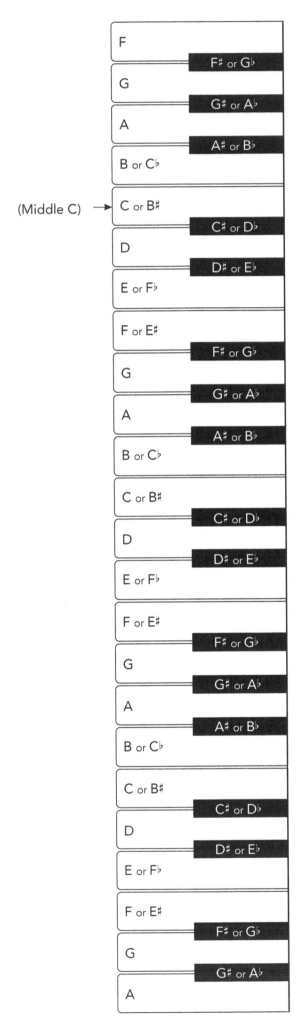

Bass and Chord Chart

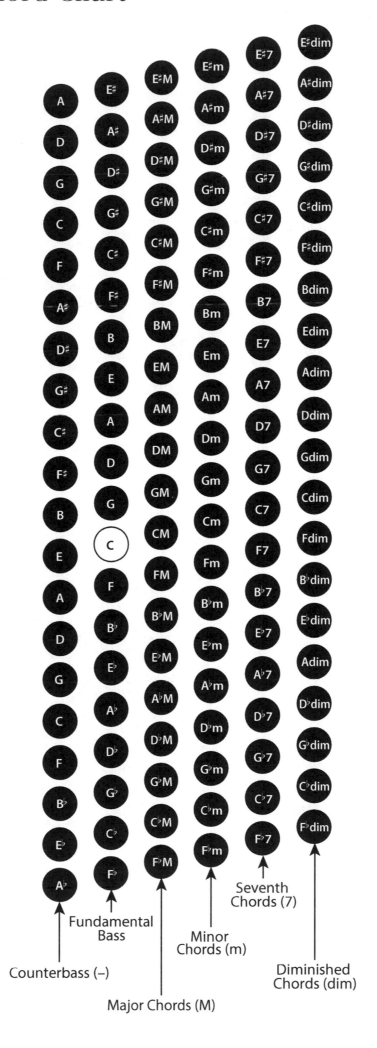

Counterbass (–)

Fundamental Bass

Major Chords (M)

Minor Chords (m)

Seventh Chords (7)

Diminished Chords (dim)

HAL•LEONARD
ACCORDION
PLAY•ALONG

The Accordion Play-Along series features custom accordion arrangements with CD tracks recorded by a live band (accordion, bass and drums). There are two audio tracks for each song – a full performance for listening, plus a separate backing track which lets you be the soloist! The CD is playable on any CD player, and is also enhanced so Mac and PC users can adjust the recording to any tempo without changing the pitch!

1. POLKA FAVORITES
arr. Gary Meisner

Beer Barrel Polka (Roll Out the Barrel) • Hoop-Dee-Doo • Hop-scotch Polka • Just Another Polka • Just Because • Pennsylvania Polka • Tic-Tock Polka • Too Fat Polka (She's Too Fat for Me).
00701705 Book/CD Pack........................ $19.99

2. ALL-TIME HITS
arr. Gary Meisner

Edelweiss • Fly Me to the Moon (In Other Words) • I Left My Heart in San Francisco • It's a Small World • Moon River • More (Ti Guarderò Nel Cuore) • Poinciana (Song of the Tree) • When I'm Sixty-Four.
00701706 Book/CD Pack........................ $19.99

3. CLASSIC SONGS
arr. Gary Meisner

Carnival of Venice • Ciribiribin • Come Back to Sorrento • Fascination (Valse Tzigane) • Funiculi, Funicula • I Love You Truly • In the Good Old Summertime • Melody of Love • Peg O' My Heart • When Irish Eyes Are Smiling.
00701707 Book/CD Pack........................ $14.99

4. CHRISTMAS SONGS
arr. Gary Meisner

Frosty the Snow Man • Have Yourself a Merry Little Christmas • Here Comes Santa Claus (Right down Santa Claus Lane) • The Most Wonderful Time of the Year • Rudolph the Red-Nosed Reindeer • Santa Claus Is Comin' to Town • Silver Bells • Winter Wonderland.
00101770 Book/CD Pack........................ $14.99

5. ITALIAN SONGS
arr. Gary Meisner

La Sorella • La Spagnola • Mattinata • 'O Sole Mio • Oh Marie • Santa Lucia • Tarantella • Vieni Sul Mar.
00101771 Book/CD Pack........................ $14.99

HAL•LEONARD®

Visit Hal Leonard online at **www.halleonard.com**

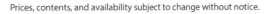